What I Know

I KNOW THE WEATHER

By Trisha James

Gareth Stevens PUBLISHING

first concepts

I know about weather.
This is a sunny day!

This is a rainy day.

This is a windy day.

This is a hot day.

This is a cold day.

This is a snowy day.

This is a cloudy day.

This is a foggy day.

This is a thunderstorm.

This is a rainbow!

What weather do you like best?